We the Consumers: What Happened to "We the People"?

It is possible to live financially free.

Stephanie A. Dickert

ISBN-13: 978-1-941749-13-5

DEDICATION

First, to my husband, for all your support and love; for my nights in frustration, your encouragement was invaluable! Thank you for walking out this book with me. Without my life with you, it wouldn't be possible. Your love gives me wings to fly.

To my beautiful daughter. I hope this is a legacy for you to live by financially so that you stay on true north and not live the school of hard knocks. Remember, it's okay to go against the grain to stay on true north.

I want to thank all of my family, for your encouragement all of my life; for instilling in me that I could do anything I wanted to do.

For the other thirteen authors who have taken this journey with me, thank you for your encouragement, love, support, and friendship! I'd especially like to thank Laura Brown, for stepping out and doing SWAT. This book would still be in the "writing" phase if you hadn't. Thank you for the accountability.

To Dr. David Banks, for that meeting so long ago and you telling me that my life wasn't over but just beginning a new chapter; for all the encouragement you've given me over the last ten years to be a leader; for showing the path that lights the way for others to follow. Thank you for pouring into me! Thank you for having a heart to see those around you succeed! Your and Sylvia's love has been the biggest gift I could ever receive!

Joe McGee, thank you for all the years of sharing about writing down your goals! I appreciate your having a life of many hats and showing me it was possible to get all that I desired and was called to accomplish; for reminding me that we are all Gideon in the beginning, but that greatness was inside of me. Go Vols!

CONTENTS

INTRODUCTION

As you start to read this, understand that I am not a radical. I am not anti-Capitalism. I am, however, in favor of responsible, controlled spending. I have spent twenty years of my life in the finance industry. I have seen it all: twenty-five-year-olds with $30,000 in credit card debt, with nothing to show for it; parents of premature twins with $50,000 in medical expenses that they did not expect; Law school graduates who have $100,000 in student loans that will take thirty years to pay off. All of them have one thing in common: they are now slaves to debt that they believe is a mountain that they will never climb.

I am so tired of looking around at a nation of people enslaved to a system that they were not designed to experience. It is my hope that this book will inspire you to see things differently; to dare to make a plan and live a good life, free of money issues; to plan for the future and live in the moment.

Money isn't a bad thing; "stuff" isn't bad. But the two, when out of control, create havoc, heartache, and health issues that we were never designed to deal with. If you are educated in your field, but don't get a "money education," you gain nothing, because no amount of money will be enough to feed the habits that our culture tells us we need. For example, culture tells us to strive to live in a big house with a high-end wardrobe. It does not tell us how big is a big house or how many clothes are enough. It just keeps telling us that we do not have enough.

We live in a country in which the founders were entrepreneurs, farmers, and business men. They did not intend for the government to fix all of our problems. They formed this nation because it was the last hope for all men and women to live freely: their original intent. None of us were designed to be enslaved to anything.

I've seen the act of planning change people's lives: parents being able to send a child to college and not have any student loan debt; people traveling the world when they are forty-five, with money coming in, due to a dream that turned into a business.

This isn't a gloom and doom book. It's a book that will provide you with a different perspective: one that shows you possibilities. We are all born with a gift and a purpose. It is up to us to find out what they are and run with them. Don't worry about doing life mistake-free. Get an education on how to handle money, and start moving. You also will notice that we, as humans, do not have eyes that go backwards. In fact, everything about us is designed to move us forward. So don't look at the past. Don't let what has happened to you in the past financially to determine your future. Failure doesn't define you; it is an incident that happens – that is all. You pick yourself up, dust yourself off, learn something from it and put it to good use.

This book isn't just about the things I've seen. It's about my life. Some of the stories I share are failures I've had and recovered from. Life is different for all of us, and if we can inspire each other along the way, it will be easier than if we were living on this planet alone. The Bible says that people perish for a lack of knowledge. So if this book imparts any knowledge to you, then I've accomplished my goal. My hope is for a country of financially educated people who live in the freedom that they were born to live in.

I desire to see this nation be truly a nation of free people – people free to be who they were born to be; free to follow their dreams and live the gift that is in them. We were all born with a silver spoon. It is that spoon that will inspire us to get to our destination. It is our gift. If I can encourage you to take the first step to live different than our culture – where money is concerned – and challenge you to become who you were meant to be, without fear, then I've left a legacy that was left to me.

I was blessed to have a grandfather who loved me enough to challenge me all the time. He challenged my political thoughts, my character, my lack of confidence, and fostered my desire to learn. My parents told me my whole life that I could be anyone I wanted to be. Being a female – although we have come a long way – was going to be a challenge. They prepared me to stand on my own merits and character, and dare to take on the world.

It is my hope that I will be the voice in your head that tells you, "You can!" and "It's okay to go against the grain." All the great people in history were thought to be nuts, so you will be in good company. Look at Noah, Christopher Columbus, Isaac Newton, and Albert Einstein. Trust me, you are in good company.

1. THE BEGINNING

Let's start at the beginning. Our Founding Fathers differed on the topics of debt and spending as much as our elected officials do today. They did all want a fiscally stable country. Some believed the intellectual aristocracy should rule the nation. (Much like what we have in office today – check out some of their family histories). Some believed that people were more likely to be happy, successful, and free to be whom they were born to be – with the government off their backs. They were not consumers. They were men who wanted to create a republic for us to live under, where we could pursue happiness and live with the unalienable rights that were God-given. We, as a nation, are so far from that original vision now.

I challenge you, the reader, to endeavor to get back to our original intent. Our Founding Fathers wanted us to live in freedom, yet, sadly, today most Americans are saddled with too much debt, and no education on how to get out of it and live in the freedom our Founding Fathers fought for us to have. When they came from England, there were so many people in "debt prisons" it wasn't funny. These prisons are where our modern-day bankruptcy comes from. We believe that the national debt being left to the next generation is a new thing, and yet, most people in "slavery" back then were in that situation because they had inherited a previous generation family member's debt. Through no fault of their own, they became enslaved to that debt and were obligated to pay it off. So debt-carryover really is nothing new.

We are born with a debt-slavery mentality. We haven't had too many examples in modern day to show us a way to live without debt. We believe that, to own something, we need to borrow money to get it, and there is no other way, because that is what our culture tells us. It's fashionable to have an American Express Gold card. It's a social status symbol. In reality, it's modern-day slavery. We take a job based on the amount of money it will pay us so that we can pay our debt, not because it is something we are passionate about and brings us fulfillment and satisfaction.

People aged twenty-one to thirty-five tend to have an overdraft, at least one credit card (often several), and a personal loan. Women are more likely to have store card and catalogue debt than men. The most common borrowing instrument is the credit card. This is followed, from most popular to least, by: personal loans, overdrafts, store cards, catalogue debt, and debt which has been sold or passed on to debt collection agencies. People under thirty-five have the highest balances on personal loans; for those over thirty-five, the highest balances are on credit cards.

While writing this book, there was an article on USA Today's website discussing the IRS seizing refunds of children and grandchildren to pay decade-old debts of their family members. Some of these debts actually go back to the 1960s but the IRS doesn't have records anymore of the debt owed. There used to be a ten-year limit on those debts, but that ban has been lifted. If this doesn't get your attention that we, as a nation, need to get a handle on money, nothing will. We are headed to repeat history if we do not become vigil about this.

The latest data tells us that, in 2013, one-million people filed bankruptcy. They filed for multiple reasons: medical bills, loss of income (job), divorce, or death of spouse. This filing is actually down from 2011 and 2012. The greatest percentage of filings are due to medical bills. Most people do not have an emergency fund or medical expense savings account to cover the unexpected things that can happen. The latest divorce statistics show that most divorces are caused by money. I see a pattern here.

Then you have our culture telling you that "stuff" is the thing to spend your money on. When you were little, did you watch the commercials during cartoons the closer it was to Christmas, or the Sears toy catalog when it came in the mail? That was a wasted day at our house. My sister and I would read it cover to cover to see what it was we wanted Santa to bring us. Santa isn't bad, mind you, but it starts there. We believe in a man who brings us stuff for free, and so begins the desensitization of our minds. We don't realize that Mom and Dad have to save or charge those "free" gifts that come from Santa.

I love Christmas; it is a wonderful time of year. Magical things happen during that season – people think of others, and usually, we go out and buy gifts for people we love – unless you are that segment of the population who participate in Christmas because you feel obligated. We should never, no matter what time of year, give out of obligation – it defeats the purpose of the true nature of giving. When I have asked people over the years, why they buy gifts, I have received many answers. Most say, "Because I know they love this [item], and they wouldn't spend their money on themselves." Others say, "I thought of them when I saw it and bought it to give it to them." So then, if we are to follow our heart and give to others, how do we do that without overspending or bankrupting ourselves?

What I have found interesting, since the downturn of the economy, is that more generosity has shown up. There was a man who walked into a K-Mart in California and asked what the total of the store's layaway was and he wrote a check, right then and there, to pay off everyone's stuff!

I will never forget the day that I overheard a mother talking to her child in a store. The child asked for something and the mother responded, "We do not have the money for that right now." The child responded, "That's okay, we can just write a check."

The older we get, the more we are told we should dress in certain clothes, we should have a certain house, and we should drive a certain car. Why? "We the People" became "We the Consumers." We gripe about our government overspending, but we are not willing to live by the standard that we expect them to live by. What would happen if "We the People" created a budget and actually lived by it? We have the Tea Party that is trying to reform the government, but what I am saying is to reform *you*, and the government will follow. It's hard to ask them to do something that we are not willing to do ourselves.

I can remember, as a sixth grader, being aware of the kids I went to school with who shopped at the Leader. It was a store that carried all the preppy clothes: Dickey pants, monogrammed everything (you know that was popular in the 80s), Sebago's and Bermuda shorts. I wanted a green pair of Dickey pants and a blue monogrammed sweater. Now, mind you, I had clothes to wear; I had nice clothes to wear – they just weren't what I wanted. I saved money until I could buy those things. I was mad at my mother for *days*, because she wouldn't let me get my initials monogrammed on the sweater. I only got to get my last name initial, so my sister could wear it later. I couldn't understand it, but that's what I did.

Today, I still like to dress in nice clothes. I shop in a store that has high price tags. Over time, I have learned how to shop that store to get the best deals. I love designer, but I don't pay designer prices. It's all about knowing how to shop.

There is a system, and if you learn the system, you can play their game – on *your* terms. As a child though, you are introduced to the system, but not told how not to become a slave to it! You just see the pictures and children around you with nice stuff. If you aren't comfortable with who you are, you begin to tell yourself you are missing something. Guess what? You aren't! You were born with everything you will ever need to succeed. You aren't missing anything. I am not a psychologist; I'm an accountant. I can tell you though, most of our spending habits are driven from our minds and emotions telling us we are missing something that we can only get from buying things.

The first young lady I worked with, opened my eyes to the problems of having a large amount of debt. After working with her, I could see, in my own life, where I was trying to fill a void with "stuff." She was twenty-five and had just graduated college. She was just hired for her first "real" job. She came into my office to get a debt consolidation loan. She was $25,000 in credit card debt. In talking to her, she had lived on credit cards while in college. She worked as a waitress to make the minimum payments, and now she wanted to put them all together and pay them off. She needed to do that to get a new car. She had been told by the car dealership that her debt-to-income ratio was too high, and that if she could consolidate her debt and get her payments down, they could finance her the car. Well, I could not do an unsecured consolidation loan for $25,000, because the institution I worked for only allowed for ten percent of your gross income, and hers didn't come close to it.

I could, however, help her in the long-term. I had her get all her debt paperwork and bring it back to my office. I showed her how, in about eighteen months, she could be out of debt. I gave her the bad news that she didn't need to purchase a new car right now; she needed to drive the "old clunker" she had so that she could get her financial future off to a good start. She was lucky – she hadn't tarnished her credit yet. As I would learn later, that is when most people begin to wake up. It's harder to fix, but it can be done.

I saw her about two years later. She had, in fact, paid off the credit card debt. She got a second job waiting tables, so she could start saving money for a house, and, in that time, she had saved almost $10,000 towards a house. I haven't seen her in years, but I'm sure she is doing fine.

She was awakened to the fact that she didn't like the slavery she felt from debt and wanted to live free.

Back to the beginning: The longer you ponder on what you see on TV, things begin to happen. You begin to think about what you don't have, you begin to say what you don't have, you begin to buy what you don't have, and the next thing you know, you're not living on a budget and you are in debt – the same as our government. We all have "seasons" in our lives: what we are capable of at that time in our life. If we live in the season we are in, everything goes well. When we try to live outside our season, bondage, stress, and worry show up.

There are still many people who are "We the Consumers" though. The Jones' raise the bar each year for them, and they run, chasing that bar, only to find it is like a mirage in the desert – unreachable.

Ben Franklin was one of our wealthy Founding Fathers. He wrote many things about money and how to handle it. He lived what he wrote. He was a living example to us. I don't recall anyone teaching Ben's money management skills when I was in school. Sadly, most parents are not teaching it to their children at home either, because there has been a disconnect in that type of education for a generation or two.

Solomon was also wise where money was concerned. He wrote a lot about money as well. He lived by what he wrote as well. He, based on historical data, lived very well too. He cautioned about money and fools. He also discussed what happens when people get money and haven't had a money education.

The generation in this nation that grew up in the Great Depression understood what it meant to "do without" and "live on less". They were forced to ask the grocer to extend credit to them for groceries when they were in dire need. Credit offers weren't mailed to them daily, and credit was not something you used for "wants." That wasn't even a concept to them. History shows that the greatest growth in housing happened between the 40s and the 60s, on the hills of the Great Depression and WWII. The "American Dream" of home ownership began in this time-frame. This was when the house with a white picket fence was born.

The definition of "enslaved" is: "To reduce to slavery or bondage: to deprive of liberty and subject to the will of a master." Sadly, most people in America are in slavery – to money and debt. Our attitude and education on money are why we are where we are today. (I will discuss attitude and education a little later.) Our Founding Fathers may be a little surprised at what we've done with what they've given us. They wanted us to live in freedom, and we do live in a free nation, but most of us are in bondage.

I'm sure, by now, you're beginning to feel like Neo from The Matrix: You mean, all of this isn't what it seems? You are correct. We've been told from the beginning that we need to have a house with a white picket fence, a nice luxury car or SUV, and $50 shirts to be considered successful. All the while, never being told that you *also* need life insurance to pay off all this stuff if something happens to you. Nor were we told that a 3000-square-foot house is expensive to heat and cool. We're just told to get this stuff so we can say we "achieved success" by the "American Dream" standard. We aren't told how to sustainably live and be ready in every season of our life, just: grow up, get an education, get a job, get stuff, and he who dies with the most stuff wins.

It's time to take the red pill and see how deep this rabbit hole goes. It's time to look at our life in a way that is different from how our culture tells us to look at it. You were born with a gift. That gift is what you're supposed to develop, to leave on this planet for the generations to come, so that they are better off than we are. What burns within you? What is the thing that you can't keep off your mind? That's probably your gift. The sooner you get to developing it, the sooner you will see your financial future and your life change.

2. IT ISN'T ALL ABOUT YOU

I know this is going to be a shock to most people, but the money you make isn't about you. Yes, you should have a roof over your head, transportation, food, and clothes on your back, but you should not be so stingy at heart that you can't do anything for your fellow neighbor. This reminds me of Mr. Scrooge. He thought he had arrived – he was successful and lived in a large house – but his employees despised him. He wanted people to work hard for him to make him more money. He didn't care about their well-being. He was loathed, and he didn't seem to care.

This is still the case today. Credit card companies want you to carry a balance to make them money. They want you to go over your limit so they can extend you more credit and keep you in bondage to their terms, interest rates, and fees – for longer. Mortgage companies want you to refinance your mortgage with them, so you can pay off your consumer debt, so they can collect interest from you for more years to come. It's a cycle.

When you refinance your home, you pay closing costs and fees. You also, usually, increase the balance, because you are trying to pay off additional debt that you have incurred. So the higher balance, the more interest that's paid to them, and for an additional number of years. We haven't been educated on that cycle. They aren't doing you any favors. They want you to increase their "bottom line" – their company's profits for the year.

Payday loans are another enslavement. This is where you borrow against your future paychecks that you will receive in the next week or two weeks. These loans are not designed to be paid off. They are designed to be refinanced over and over so that you continue to make them money. It's time to see all of this for what it is: The Matrix – a system that was designed to fool us, not educate us.

Back to Scrooge. His workers and neighbors detested him. It is ironic that he was haunted because of his life. If we cannot help out our neighbors, what good are we? We should be able to lend a hand to someone in need. I am not saying to give to every person standing on the side of the road. You need to be wise to people who scam others, but if you know your neighbor has been laid off, what an awesome gift to buy them groceries or pay their house payment.

How do you define success? To me, it's being able to leave money behind when you are gone to allow the next generation to have it better than you did. What would it be like to leave a legacy like Bill and Melinda Gates have done with the "Bill & Melinda Gates Foundation"?

The difference between "We the People" and "We the Consumers" is greatest when it comes to leaving a legacy.

When this country was first founded, we helped each other harvest their crops and clear land. Life was about community. We were mindful of each other, and we helped each other through life. Today, we won't walk across the street to ask our neighbor how they are – if we even know who our neighbors are. I know, as a child, when someone had a death in the family, neighbors took food to that family for weeks. Now, if someone takes one meal, it's a miracle.

We need to ask ourselves why we are so worried about ourselves and no one else. Why is it that when 9/11 happened, we flooded the blood banks and churches, and within one month, we were back to business as usual. How sad it is that it took something tragic to get our attention. Then it did not keep our attention.

What would our world look like if we looked outside ourselves and lent a helping hand to our neighbors? Greater than that, what would happen if we taught the next generation to think of others? I'm not suggesting that we join the Peace Corps – just look around your neighborhood and see where you can make a difference.

I volunteer with several nonprofit organizations. I am *amazed* at the lack of participation in our communities. The boards I serve on have to beg and plead to get people to serve, and when they do, most are doing it out of obligation. What if we did it because we were passionate about the organization? In my case, accounting is one of my gifts; it comes naturally to me. Because of that, I believe it is my duty to help my community nonprofits be all that they can be financially. It's also why I decided to run for office. I have a gift that can help my community.

We complain about the current political situation, but we do not step up to run. Why? We don't help others to run. Maybe being in office isn't your thing, but helping someone you trust get into office, who can make a difference, is just as important. Voting, for sure, is important. Thomas Jefferson once said, "Science is my passion, politics my duty." We have a critical role to play in our political system. It is amazing, to me, how we take that for granted. We are enslaved to money, and we are so focused on making money, that we don't take the time to vote. What if we lived in the time when, as a slave, we couldn't vote? Would we feel different about it then?

The legislation that was passed in the last decade, where money is concerned – the new housing bill that allows lenders to "forgive" part of your debt if you are upside-down on your loan, and involves equity sharing, which most people don't understand or aren't aware of – has had adverse effects on us (another book unto itself), and no one paid attention to it when it was being passed. We were too busy getting up, going to work, paying bills, going to bed, and repeating the same cycle over and over.

According to volunteeringinamerica.org, my home state of Georgia ranks 40th out of 50 in America for volunteering. Only 24% of our citizens volunteer in their community. And only 49% of the population gives to a charity. What is the number one state you might ask? Utah. They have 43% who volunteer and 70% who give to charity. The startling thing in the data they provide: the percentage of people who volunteer is, on average, over fifty-five years old. There appears to be a disconnect between the younger generation and their communities.

Across the nation, there is a new concept in schools from when I was in school: parents are asked to volunteer so many hours a year to their child's school. A school teacher friend says it is like pulling teeth to get the parents into the school. My question to the parents is: why aren't you willing to volunteer? You may see something that you can do to help revolutionize the education system.

If for no other reason, here are some reasons to volunteer and give out of yourself: studies have shown an increase in morality, it can lower your blood pressure, you can learn new skills, and it sets a good example for the next generation.

The wealthiest people in this country – think Warren Buffet and Bill Gates – give away large sums of money every year. It's a funny thing about them: they give away money, they make more money, they give away money, they make more money. See the pattern?

Look, it boils down to this: if you do the same thing over and over and expect a different result, that's called insanity. If we want to live a different existence, we need to make some changes. Step one: give out of yourself. Period.

If you can make the leap to see your financial future as more than you, it will change forever the way your money flows to you. Here's visualization for you: when a pipe has water flowing through it, it still gets wet. So see yourself as that pipe. You never know when giving out of yourself will open a door that will "water" your financial future. Anything is possible.

Have you ever had anyone say that "attitude is everything"? Well, with money, it really is. If you have the wrong attitude about money, you will repel it from you – not attract it to you. If you live in chaos, and are unorganized, you will repel money from yourself. Chaos will cause "paycheck to paycheck" living. Most people don't have an issue with their money paying the bills; it's a lack of organization that causes late payments. Now, I'm not saying that is always the case, but in my experience, that has been the issue more times than not. If you have the attitude that everything is about you, money will repel from you.

I want to address the "entitlement attitude" for a moment. There was a news story recently about a young lady who sued her parents for tuition and financial support. I cannot imagine how this would have ended for me had I done something like this. The judge, in this case, ruled with the parents, as I believe he should have. My siblings and I were raised that you are a part of a unit. You support each other. We were not paid an allowance. We were expected to keep our rooms clean, and our laundry sorted, until we were old enough to do our laundry on our own. We were to keep our bathroom – which happened to be the guest bath at our house – clean as well, in case we had company.

We were given a strong work ethic, and taught that character in you and how you behaved and treated others was important. You weren't put on this earth to be a taker. You were not going to get anything for free. You weren't promised anything.

We were provided a roof over our head, clothes to wear, and loving parents who cared enough to snatch us up when we acted like we were entitled to anything. Don't get me wrong, my parents gave us what was within their power to give us – not because we demanded it, but because they wanted to. I can just hear my dad now if I had demanded that he pay for or buy me anything. It would have gone something like the infamous quote from

Bill Cosby: "I brought you in this world, and I can take you out and make another just like you."

Remember I told you that I wanted clothes from the Leader? Well, I got them, when I worked and bought them myself. People think the "X" generation's sense of entitlement is something new. Every generation has had it; it's just that the older generation dealt with it. We were taught to help each other out. We were taught to take care of our family and neighbors whenever humanly possible.

There is a movie called the "Ultimate Gift." I recommend that everyone see the movie. It is a story about a young man who's given a series of gifts – the gift of work, the gift of friendship, the gift of money, the gift of love, the gift of problems, the gift of dreams (just to name a few) – by his deceased grandfather. These are the kinds of gifts we should all be leaving to the next generation.

The greatest disservice we are doing to kids today is letting them think they don't have to work for something. We are robbing them of the sense of satisfaction of a job well done – for that matter, a job done at all. Statistics tell us that the current generation is suffering from more depression than any other before it. I truly believe this is because they have not been given any expectations. We, as a nation, have become so busy keeping up with each other that we have forgotten to have goals. We all need goals; it's what makes us human. We weren't put on this planet to only consume air, but to take our individual gifts and leave it for the next generation to build upon. We are to leave the next generation better than the one before.

What is happening today is the opposite. Again, statistics show that the current generation is poised to have a shorter lifespan than the generation before, because of our eating habits, and the disease that goes along with those habits, due to us following the ways of this culture. How sad. It isn't too late to correct this, but it's going to take effort. It's going to take some sacrifice. But just think what an awesome legacy they will leave. It will be worth it to those who take on the challenge.

Working with small businesses, I hear owners tell me how hard it is to find people willing to work hard. They struggle to find people who are willing to do the job they were hired to do. One owner said he'd just be happy if his employees showed up on time. If the employee doesn't show up on time, the business may have to open late. It may also have a policy that if you show up late, you will be fired, and that will affect both the business and the employee. The business will have loss of revenue, due to employee shortage and not being able to service its customers, and the employee will have lack of income. What has caused this shift? I believe it all falls back to money. Parents kill themselves to give their kids everything they want, most of the time, as a sign that they love their kids. That isn't love. Teaching them how to handle money is love. Spending time with them is love. Not breaking your back to put them in every sport, designer clothes, and every new fad that comes along is love.

Children watch those around them. If you desire to give your child a leg up, teach them discipline, show them character, and teach them how to be a person of their word. In the work environment today, that will cause them to stand out. The values that we give to our children transfer on to the next generation. Again, businesses are looking for people who will show up on time, work while they are on the clock, and do the job they were hired to do. They are looking for employees who don't steal and who don't complain but are problem solvers. If we can teach that to our children, we will give them a skill that will give them a lifetime of good fortune.

I remember as a kid that going out to eat was a treat. We got to go to "Shake's Pizza" and have a "Federal Bake Shop" cake on our birthdays. That was huge to us. So was the time my dad took us flying with him as he worked to get his pilot's license. We thought it was awesome to get to picnic next to the plane at the little airport he flew to on a cross-country flight. The times that my mom made us sandwiches and we hiked to Point Park on Lookout Mountain as a family were also memorable. Money didn't make the memory; being with family and learning about something new did. We weren't rich, but we had a blast. On that same note, we were taught the importance of having a clean house and clothes, responsibility, and discipline – the things that I needed to be a good citizen, employee, and human being. I was encouraged to explore everything around me. I was expected to finish what I started. I was given the vision that I could become anything that I chose to be. Just some food for thought.

Today, one of the popular things to do is to trace your family tree. I was very intrigued to find out that my ancestors were business owners. One served for Thomas Jefferson while he was President. One was in the Virginia House of Burgess. We have royalty in our line and authors. So, to say that DNA just determines your physical traits, to me, is funny. As I began to learn these things, I began to become more comfortable in my own skin. I wasn't weird because I had a desire to be a public servant in my community – it was in my bloodline! My entrepreneurial mind was in my DNA! These are the kind of things you can't learn in school. They are born in you, and the generation before imparts their wisdom to you. Somewhere along the way, we, as a nation, have failed to continue this. Every culture on this planet has shared their history with the next generations. Those cultures, who have survived, have done it well and encouraged every generation to make it better. If we desire to remain free, and get off this slope of enslavement that we are on, we have to start with us, and then train the next generation how to handle money well.

I am reminded of a story from my banking days. There was an older man who came to our branch regularly to get money. He was illiterate. He signed his name with an "X." He had no idea if people were cheating him when he paid for something. We felt so sorry for him. We – me and my co-workers at the branch – created a chart for him to learn. I also think of the times I've purchased something for, say, $10.86 and I've given the clerk $20.86 to pay for it. I am always amazed when they can't count the change back. Again, this is something that we need to be teaching the next generation. It isn't being taught in school, and we should hold that responsibility as a privilege to pass on, not relying on the school system to do it for us.

3. IS IT THE RIGHT SEASON?

What if we really understood the difference between a want and a need? I am not a radical. I am not "anti-stuff." I am not for being in bondage for the next ten or twenty years to pay off something that will have no value when it's over.

We have basic needs. We need a roof over our head, food to eat, clothing to protect us from the elements, and a way to get around (transportation). We should plan for emergencies and a time when we will choose to no longer work. We the People should be the masters of our fate, captains of our souls (Winston Churchill). What would happen if we stopped pointing the finger at everyone else for our issues and looked at the man in the mirror, and made some changes? We mouth about Congress having out-of-control spending and not living on a balanced budget. What if "We the People" set the example? It only takes ten percent of the population to start a Revolution. It took fifty-two men to change the course of our history. Why can't "We the People" not do that now? Why have we allowed ourselves to become “We the Consumers”? We are never satisfied. We aren’t satisfied with our wardrobes, our cars, or our homes. When did we buy into the lie that we must have the newest and latest gadgets to be satisfied? Are we so insecure in ourselves that we need those things to make us feel whole?

I am anti living with things that it isn’t your time to have. If you can’t pay for it, it isn’t your time to have it. What happened to the days of save money, and when you have enough, buy that purchase? If you have ever done this, there is such satisfaction in having saved for an item when you finally have enough money to buy it. Taking the time to do this will help stop impulse buying.

We can’t live with the “lottery mentality.” You know: when I win the lottery, I will… (fill in the blank). Google “the lottery curse.” It’s eye opening. Most people are worse off within two years of winning the lottery than they were prior to. Why? They don’t have a plan. They impulse-buy stuff. They run through the money, because they didn’t know how to handle it. Money is the great magnifier. It shows who you really are. If you were stingy before you got it, you’ll be stingy with it. If you were a giver before, you will be a giver with it. You can have the things you imagine – with planning. You don’t need the lottery to get to that point.

When we look at what it takes to live, we begin to see what is important. Let’s review those needs once more: a roof over our head, food to eat, clothing, and transportation. People ask me all the time: “What is most important?” I tell them that all of them are. Everything above them is a want.

Roof over our head

Before the mortgage crash, you could borrow a higher percentage of your income to obtain a house than you can now. Now, the general rule of thumb is no more than 25 to 30%. If you can't buy the house you are looking at and finance it on a traditional mortgage for fifteen to thirty years, then it isn't your season for that house. Do not compromise your financial health to have the house of your dreams. It will come; it may just not be right now. "Rent or buy?" is another question I am asked. That is also about your season. Buying a house is a big responsibility. You are responsible for the leaks, breaks, and maintenance. When you rent, those things are usually covered in your rent.

Part of the American Dream is owning a home of your own. We have seen, in the last few years, "We the People" living out of their season and ending up in foreclosure, because they didn't play the game by the rules. We financed homes we could never afford on interest-only loans that came crashing down around us. We were warned. Our parents and grandparents tried to tell us how they did it when they were in our shoes. Just as our Forefathers told us what a responsibility it was for us to live free in a free nation, we, in our need to satisfy our wants, didn't heed the warning and we ended up in trouble.

You need several things before a home purchase. You need money set aside for repairs. They will come, and a home equity loan is not the answer for those. If you can't afford the heating/cooling bill for the home you are looking at, it isn't your season for that house. If you have to eat rice and beans or ramen noodles to make the mortgage payment, it isn't your season for that house.

Make sure that you have a home inspection completed, on any perspective home, by a certified home inspector. Trust me on this one; it may save you time, money, and heartache. If you choose to have a high deductible on your insurance policy, make sure you have that deductible amount in an account set aside. If you had been a renter prior to your home purchase, make sure you have lawn equipment for lawn maintenance, or money each month to pay for lawn maintenance. Furnishings – this one gets most of us into trouble. I know we'd all love to move into a new house with it fully furnished. That may or may not happen. Our taste changes over time, so it really is okay to move into a home without it being completely decorated.

I remember when I built my first house. I had a vision in my head for how beautiful my house would be. I could see it finished and decorated. Well, the cost to build was underestimated by about $20,000 and that was my budget for furnishings. So guess what? I got to move in without it finished. I was heartbroken. I wanted a house that I could be proud to invite people over and have parties. Instead, what I got to do was go room to room and furnish it one at a time. I made a list of each room and what I wanted for that room. It's amazing – in about eighteen months, I had it the way I wanted it. This little exercise was a great way for me to see what I really wanted to spend my money on. Every time I thought about eating out or buying anything other than necessities, I had a decision to make: spend money on that or on getting my house the way I wanted it. Remember, I said this was my first house. I also said it was over $20,000. Prior to this house, I had not paid rent in seven years or had *any* form of house payment. So it was a huge deal for me. It was also a reality check that you should not go above 25 to 30% of your income for the mortgage payment.

At the time that I'm writing this book, the New York Times published an article about "rent crisis." The rise in rent is causing people to spend, sometimes, up to forty percent of their income on a place to live. This is being driven by the number of people who are not renting, and instead purchasing housing. It's also because of supply and demand. We have more of a demand than we do a supply of places to live.

We also have the greatest amount of generations living together since the Great Depression. Many children graduate college and are unable to find a job. So they move back home to live with Mom and Dad. This is not the only reason families are moving in together. Some are because of health problems with their parents and some are simply to save money.

When I went through a divorce in 2001, I moved in with my parents for ninety days, until I could either buy a house or get into an apartment. I opted to move into an apartment until I could purchase a home. It was very awkward moving home. It was emotionally hard for me. Here I was a college graduate, and moving home felt like such a failure. I was the oldest dog-gone-it. I was the one who had always been responsible and had it together. Now I was feeling irresponsible and afraid. Within six months of moving into an apartment, I had found a home that was affordable, and moved from the apartment into the home. I am glad I did it the way that I did. The six months gave me time to get back on my feet and begin to gain some confidence back.

Transportation

Everyone needs it. It's a mode of getting around. Notice that I didn't say it was a 600 Series BMW. Your transportation is, again, determined by what season you are in. A car is not a status symbol. It's a way of getting from point A to point B. Depending on where you are in the country, you may have never owned a car. Your mode of transportation may be public transportation. When I was in Europe in 2006, I was amazed at the number of people who walked to the store and to work. Their trains travel at high speeds, and they do not have to worry about the price of fuel or insurance costs. Here in the States, we think about those things, because we are a little more spread apart than they are, so some of us would have to walk or bike over twenty miles to get to the nearest grocery store.

I love the new communities that are being built. They are including a gym, store, and restaurant in the "commons" of the community – no driving is necessary. Again, when purchasing an automobile, think about the future. Have a down-payment already saved. Have money set aside in an account for repairs, so they don't strain you financially. Depending on the year, make, and model, insurance will be different rates as well. And don't forget that our past driving record affects that as well. So make sure to research how much your insurance payments will be and make sure that you can afford them – and all other car-related expenses – before purchasing a vehicle.

The bottom line on transportation: a paid for car is cheaper than a new car most of the time. So what if it isn't brand new? Remember, it doesn't reflect who you are. It just moves you around.

Clothing

This one gets me more dirty looks than any other item. Buy quality clothing that you can budget. If your budget allows Armani, then by all means get it. If you can't budget for Armani, then find a quality product that you can. Look – if it is clean, pressed, and fits, no one is going to ask you what label you are wearing. Our clothes don't make it forty years; they will come and go. So get quality items that you like and move on. Who you're wearing isn't nearly as important as how it looks on you, and whether or not you are enslaved to a department store – or major creditor – to have it on.

I can remember my first job like it was yesterday. I was working in banking and I needed some "business" attire, but I owned nothing like that. I remember going shopping and getting sticker-shock over the prices of suits and dress clothes for women. Hose – I *hate* them. In that day, we had to wear them if we were wearing a skirt. They were expensive to someone making a whopping $12,000 a year. And they tore easily. That is how I began to learn how to shop stores thriftily. We used to go to Richs' bargain basement in downtown Atlanta. It had last year's items or ones that were "seconds" – not first quality. I purchased three basic suits that were pants or skirts, and jackets. Then all I needed to do was change my blouses and accessories, and each outfit was different. Not as easy as men, mind you – they change a tie and no one is the wiser.

Recently, there was a group of people who took a challenge called "six items or less." These folks took six items from their wardrobe and wore them for thirty days. Now, you could have unlimited accessories and shoes, but you could only have six basic pieces. Do you know what they found? Most of their co-workers didn't notice until about day twenty. And we worry about wearing the same dress as "so and so" to a party. We are not as observant as we like to think we are. For pity's sake, it usually takes us a few days to realize that Bob shaved his beard or that Mary changed the style or color of her hair. Buy what you feel comfortable in, that you can budget, and keep moving.

Food

This is another one that gets me looks. Fast food is the *worst* thing you can eat. I don't care how many of "them" try to tell us otherwise – it is! If you eat too much of anything, it's a bad thing. We, as a culture, eat out more now than we have in the history of our nation. We are also the most unhealthy that we have ever been. We medicate ourselves for more stuff than should be allowed by law. We don't sleep, because of the caffeine we give ourselves and the worry we put ourselves through. We are consuming so much that we don't even stop to think what we are putting in our mouths anymore.

If we want to truly get back to "We the People," we are going to have to make some healthy decisions about our lives to get us there. These will not be easy decisions. The narrow road is always harder, but in the end, it will make all the difference.

Buy as much natural, local food as you can fit into your budget. A good friend of mine owns a "lifestyle changing" fitness studio. She gives tours of grocery stores. She will tell you to only shop the perimeters of the store. You know – where the fruits, vegetables, meat, and dairy are. Not the center aisles with the cookies and pre-packed meals – loaded with crap that you can't pronounce. If you would take the time to go to your pantry and google some of the ingredients, you would be horrified. I do my very best to buy from our local organic grocery store. I shop the sales and stock up on items that can be frozen. I also buy local-grown produce and meat whenever possible. I eat out too. Again, I am not radical. I am, however, choosy where I eat. I do not eat fast food, unless it is an absolute last resort.

I have found that it costs just as much to eat bad as it does to eat well. Our country was founded on people farming. Until we began to put our farmers out of business, we could get lettuce grown here in the US, not Mexico. We used to be a nation that produced our own crops and meat. If we don't stop being "We the Consumers," gardens and farms will be a thing of the past. Rebel – grow a backyard or window garden with your favorite fruit and veggies.

Speaking of farming, let me finish this chapter by addressing seasons. We all go through our own personal seasons. Our planet goes through its environmental seasons. It isn't a bad thing. It's natural. We can't get strawberries all year, unless they are grown in a greenhouse, because their season only happens briefly once a year. We can't get pumpkins all year either. The same is true with the seasons in our personal lives.

We have seasons of gathering. We put up for the "winter" – or the "lean" times that we may experience. This is what I'm talking about when I say you need an account with money for car breakdowns. You also should have an account with three to six months of expenses, in case you have a time when you are not able to work. We end up in trouble when we don't gather.

We have a planting season. We sow into other people's lives. That doesn't mean just during Christmas. We should give of ourselves all year 'round. It is part of what makes us whole and satisfied people. We create a budget and we live by it. We "plant" in every area on that budget: retirement, college fund, house fund, car fund. Don't miss this; it will change your life: If you look back in our history at the people who made it through the Great Depression, they were people who lived within their means. I learned some unique things about Jewish people in the 70s and 80s. When their country went to war, Jews all over the world went from driving two cars and having summer houses to selling those luxuries in order to send money to their fellow Jews, so they could fight for their existence.

We have a reaping season. This is the hardest for most people to deal with. It is harder to receive than to give. It will come, and you should say "thank you" and keep moving. This may also come in the form of people seeing your gift and expertise and paying you to help them. It may come in the form of an idea that is purchased from you to change the world. Don't sell yourself short. Know what you are worth. Don't despise small beginnings (everyone starts somewhere), but as Suze Orman says, "Don't put yourself on sale." In other words, don't apologize for what you charge for your time. You have value, and the sooner you see it, so will those around you.

We have a resting season. This is when we stay with the plan we have put in place and work that plan without any movement to the right or the left. Don't think you've arrived. You've just hit the plateau before the final ascent to the mountain top. This is a time of "breathing room." This may be when you decide to set up a foundation to help out what you are passionate about. It is my goal to have two foundations: one that helps students go to college expense-free or start their own business, and one that helps out people who want to farm. In regards to the first one, I think student loans are a way to enslave someone for many years to come, in order for them to receive an education. Student loans are not the answer. In regards to the farming foundation, the federal government offers some programs for new farmers, but not enough. Again, farm loans are not the way to start out a new operation. My desire to start these two foundations comes from my belief of what I said earlier: giving out of yourself.

I want to share a story with you about planning. There is a successful businessman I know, who was married with three children. He had life insurance on himself, but not on his wife. His wife died within days of giving birth to their fourth child – from an aneurism. Why is that an issue? He's now a single dad with a company to run, and three school-age children and an infant. He had to hire a nanny. He said he didn't carry insurance on his wife because she didn't work – she didn't bring in any income that might need to be supplemented. Well, she had worked, and now he is paying for her job to be done. Had he had a life insurance policy for her, it may have paid for his nanny. I tell you this story, because in planning for the future, everything should be considered. You may clean your house yourself. What would happen if you were incapacitated for a season? Who is going to clean your house and cook the food? That has a cost associated to it.

I am frequently asked about retirement. How much should I put away and how should I invest retirement money? Find a reputable investor. Take a class at your local college in the continuing education department about retirement investing. Whatever you do, just do it.

Plan for retirement. In case you aren't aware, social security will not take care of you. You should have money that is before and after tax money – money that helps you on taxes now (gives you a deduction), and money that has already had tax paid on it to invest. I am not going to go into detail about that in this book. A licensed investor can help you with how much, and what percentage, you should set aside for each.

As far as seasons go, if you skip over a season or you try to live in a season that you are not in, life will be hard. You will not have peace, joy, or sleep. Trust me on this one. Be happy in whatever season you are in and know that it is just that – a season. Seasons come and go. They do not last for an eternity. It may feel, right now, like you are in an eternal part of your life, but I promise, it will change. The one thing we are assured of in this life is that things change.

Let me give you a visual for different seasons. Take ants – they gather for the winter; they prepare for what is coming. Ants build a home, protect their young, feed themselves, and plan for the winter that will come. They will need to eat in the winter. If you observe an ant hill, they are always busy with something: cleaning out the hill, bringing in food, and caring for their eggs that will bear baby ants that will need to be fed and taught what to do as they mature. Then take locusts – they consume everything in their way. They show up every so many years (there are different cycles) and they wreak havoc while they are around, not to mention the noise they bring with them.

So how do you see yourself at this point in your life? Do you consume everything around you and make lots of noise while you do it? Do you plan for the future and train the next generation to do better than you did? I am not judging you here. Rather, I want you to think about how you're living your life and achieve what you desire out of life. Remember how I said earlier that it starts with the man in the mirror? It is most important to regularly take an inventory of where you are. What season are you in? Where are you financially? How do you eat an elephant? One bite at a time.

I have had the privilege of speaking to young people about starting out their financial adult life better than I did. In listening to them, they talk about the founder of Facebook and how he is young and wealthy. My comments to them on that is: not everyone will have that happen to them. Just like not all people will make a six-figure salary playing sports. I get their attention when I tell them that they could retire as a millionaire, on a minimum wage job, if they make a plan and work the plan.

Anyone can have a bright financial future. Look, not everyone wins the lottery. The chances of it happening are slim. So instead of leaving everything to chance, focus on what you want in your future and move in that direction.

4. IT'S ABOUT THE PLAN

I mentioned in an earlier chapter about how much to spend and to plan for things. Here's the rest of that story.

Every single person and business on this planet needs a budget. That drives everything else. Can I take a job with less income but in the field I am passionate about? Your budget will tell you what you need to live on. It's nothing more than a road map. It isn't shackles or a restriction. When we see it for what it is, we don't dread it. It really is one of the most freeing things you will do for yourself and/or your business.

Most people don't realize this. You get a report card all your life. When you get out of school, it is called a balance sheet. It shows what you own versus what you owe. If you owe more than you own, well, that's like getting a D in school in a subject. Just like in school, you can improve your "grades" on your balance sheet. The first step is with a budget.

What is a budget? Well, I'm glad you asked. It is simply how much you make minus how much you need to pay out. A balanced budget means you have a place to spend or save or invest every single dime you make. This is why it's so important: it will help you stop the compulsive spending. If you already have your money spent, then when you see that pair of Jimmy Chu shoes that you want, you will, with confidence, say, "This isn't the season for that, because I didn't budget for them."

Why else keep a budget? It keeps you focused on your goals. If you have a goal to retire in ten years with one million dollars to live on, and you budget for that, then you will think twice about spending that budget item on something else. You have set a goal, and just writing it down makes it fifty percent more likely to happen, according to researchers. It's the same with using cash versus plastic to pay for purchases. There is a chemical reaction that happens when we hand over cash to purchase something that does not happen when we use a debit or credit card. Ever wonder why, when that monthly credit card bill comes, you are surprised by the balance? Focus is the great equalizer. It helps us realize our goals. Without it, we are a shotgun being fired, where our efforts are scattered. But with it, we are a rifle that hits the target every time.

Having a budget involves discipline. When you make the decision to create and live by a budget, you are disciplining yourself to not just waste money and consume things. You are calculated and deliberate with your purchases. You create a road map for your life and you live by it. Yes, that map will change over time, and you will need to adjust to it, but you will never be without it.

Our Founding Fathers created the Constitution as a road map for our nation. They were disciplined about it. They saw the importance of having direction for where the nation would go. They covered most of the bases for everything that should have been addressed or could come up for us as a nation, as the constitution has been altered very little since its original signing. They knew the importance of anticipating issues that may arise and having a plan to address them.

Can you imagine starting out on a trip without a map or GPS? You want to go to California and you're in New York. You could end up in Canada without the direction of a map or GPS. You'll find yourself sounding like Bugs Bunny: "I should have made that turn at Albuquerque."

You don't want to wake up at sixty-five with part of your life over and nothing to show for it. Tomorrow is a new day, and you can start this at any time and make your life all that you want it to be.

So what's needed for a budget and what are the basics? They are as follows:

Income: You should list, after taxes, what you have to spend. Do not count bonus or commission income, as it may not be regular.

Expenses:

Giving – Gifts, to charitable organizations, to someone in need.

Savings – *Pay yourself first!* Have three to six months in expenses put away, retirement, college fund, wish list (things you'd like to have – wants).

Insurance – Life and health.

Living expenses – House/rent payment, insurance, utilities, security system, repairs/maintenance, property taxes.

Food – Groceries and eating out.

Transportation – If you have an automobile: gasoline, insurance, maintenance, tags, payment if financed. Otherwise: money for public transportation.

Utilities – Electricity, gas, cable, phone.

Personal – Hair care, clothing, well visits, emergencies, gym membership, sports membership, vacation.

Debt – Get this paid off!

You should be able to live on less than you make. When you start adding debt – to live out of season – or not following your budget, then you begin to get in trouble. As you start this process, remember: Rome wasn't built in a day but it was built. Slow and steady wins the race. You may have debt to pay off in your first budget. As time moves on and you discipline yourself, you will see your budget change to what you envision your life to be.

I'm a visual person. It helps me to be able to picture something to really get it. With that in mind, let me see if I can paint a picture for you. When a runner begins to train for a race, they don't run the full distance the first time. They start out running a mile. Then two. They continue to train and expand their time and distance until they reach their goal. If a runner was going to run a marathon (26.2 miles) and ran the whole distance in a day, I'm sure that runner would have a hard time moving the next day, as their body was not used to the distance or stress on their body. Same with getting your finances in order. If your budget doesn't look like you want it to the first month, don't give up. Keep at it. Disciplined is defined as: "Instructed; educated; subjected to rules and regulations." That means doing the right thing the first time, every time – period. A runner is disciplined to eat right, and train until it's time to run the race. You are training for the run of your life: your financial life.

I grew up an athlete, and discipline has always been a part of my life. I know what it feels like to push for a goal. The story I'm going to tell you isn't meant to bash anyone. When I was in my twenties, I got married. This was my first experience of dealing with someone else where money was concerned. He had not ever lived on his own where he had to deal with rent and living expenses. He had lived on his own, but he was away at school and all his expenses were paid. Before we got married, I had lived on my own. I was making a whopping 12,000 a year and had rent, car payment, food, and clothing to pay for, and wanted to have some fun too. All work and no play makes Jack a dull boy. I didn't have the experience with money that I do now. My parents didn't talk to me about money. I knew my mom was a stay-at-home mom and we weren't made of money. I knew we went to the grocery store and spent $700.00 a month to feed five of us. I remember going to Crossville Tennessee to get green beans so we could can them. My grandfather grew up in the Great Depression and he never financed anything in his life. If he couldn't pay cash for it, he didn't buy it.

In contrast, my husband had never had to pay bills. Prior to him going to school, his mom helped him with his finances. So when we got together, it was kind of a mess.

We were very different when it came to money and that put stress on our relationship. We didn't pay rent; we lived in an apartment below my in-laws. Having been on my own, that was hard. I wanted our own place. I wanted a house. We built a house. A beautiful one. We didn't get to do that until we got our plan together and started living it. Before the house was finished though, we ran out of money and had to borrow from our families to finish it. I wasn't sure how we were going to pay that money back and make it. Why had the house cost us more than we had thought? Instead of coming together as a team, I blamed him for the mess, and that began the breakdown of our relationship. Eventually it ended in divorce. I lived in the house for three years, and then had to start all over again. I had to put my pride down. I moved into an apartment. Not only was I dealing with the emotional issues of having a divorce, but I had to create a new plan and start a new chapter of my life. Within six months, I bought a house. I began to pick myself back up. Where I was, at thirty-two, was not where my plan said I should be. I was supposed to be on my way to retirement and having a family – not starting all over. So when I tell you it is possible to survive anything, I mean it.

Take the time to make the plan, and stick to it. Roll with the punches. If you have to start over, don't be afraid; just do it.

Fast forward to me at 34. I got remarried. Before I got married, I did things a little different than the first time. We talked about *everything.* I asked about his money habits. He had been divorced and had been on his own for five years. We had similar thoughts about money. We had different goals where money was concerned, but we discussed those and we came to a compromise so that we both could achieve our goals. We haven't reached them all yet, but we have a plan and we are working it. Let me add this: we haven't been without bumps in the road. We've had to alter our plan several times in the eight years that we have been married. We've done it as a team.

While I'm talking about this, if you are single and reading this, before you marry anyone, make sure you discuss money. Trust me when I say, it will be the difference between a happy marriage and heartache. If you are married and find yourself fighting about money all the time, please, sit down and make a plan. It may not be what you both want at the moment, but it will set you on a disciplined path that will get you to where you both want to go. Not talking about it will not make it better, and fighting and laying blame will not make it better either. If you can't sit down together and talk about it, find a local money management class and go.

Creating a plan will take the emotion out of money for you. You will have a calculated vision of where you want to go and how you want to get there. It will help you to not feel the need to keep up with the Jones'.

Let's go back to our Founding Fathers for a moment. The Bill of Rights and the Constitution were plans for the country. The Founders wrote those to set the country on a course for things to be different in America than they had been in England. They looked at where they wanted the country to be in the years to come, and they put their plan into motion. Now is your opportunity to create a plan and put it into motion.

Let me just share with you this: The last few months, I've been blessed with the opportunity to speak to high school seniors and work-study students. I can't tell you what a rush it is to see this next generation get it. In twenty minutes, we go through what we need money for and how to create a budget. We actually create one in those twenty minutes. I ask them if it hurt to do it. Most said, "No." Others said, "We didn't' know we'd have to do math," to which I laughed. I'm sharing this with you, because if they can get it in twenty minutes, we can all do it.

Again, a budget isn't an evil thing – it's a road map. If you will take the time to set it up, you'll be amazed at how soon you'll begin to see the financial future that you desire. The next page shows a budget. It is available for download on my website: www.stewardshipforlife.net.

The next few pages will give you some reality checks on things we spend money on.

Expense	Today	For 10 years	For 30 years
Pizza Delivery	$25 a week	$18,661	$158,731
Coffee, Donut	$4 a day	$22,389	$190,453
Smoking	$35 a week	$25,125	$222,223
Manicure	$40 a week	$29,857	$253,969
Lunch at work	$5 a day	$13,000	$195,000
Golf	$75 a week	$55,983	$634,924

The chart above may be a little shocking. But it illustrates that, if you spend your money right, you can retire a millionaire on any income. If you just eliminate the weekly manicure, you could put aside that money and, over thirty years, look at what you will have saved. See how easy it would be to do? Just $40.00 a week. Really, it isn't rocket science. Just as a disclaimer, I'm not saying never get a manicure. I simply want to give you the hope that it is possible to save money, and lots of it, with a plan.

I am sure there are items in this chart that you could do a comparison on. Think about the pizza delivery one. Forget about the money you could save, for a minute. Think, instead, about the amount of time it would take for you to make a pizza with your significant other or family. Think of the memories you will be building, and the opportunity to teach someone the joy of cooking and making something yourself. Some of my favorite memories as a child are of our family cooking in the kitchen together – the Christmas cookies that we made, or the Easter eggs that we dipped and dyed. I remember, in fifth grade, my 4H competition, when my mom helped me make biscuits. I got second place. Talk about a confidence builder. I remember her saying, "Don't handle them too much; you'll make them tough." It isn't always about the money.

52-Week Saving Challenge

Week	Amount to Deposit	Balance		Week	Amount to Deposit	Balance
1	1.00	1.00		27	27.00	378.00
2	2.00	3.00		28	28.00	406.00
3	3.00	6.00		29	29.00	435.00
4	4.00	10.00		30	30.00	465.00
5	5.00	15.00		31	31.00	496.00
6	6.00	21.00		32	32.00	528.00
7	7.00	28.00		33	33.00	561.00
8	8.00	36.00		34	34.00	595.00
9	9.00	45.00		35	35.0	630.00
10	10.00	55.00		36	36.00	666.00
11	11.00	66.00		37	37.00	703.00
12	12.00	78.00		38	38.00	741.00
13	13.00	91.00		39	39.00	780.00
14	14.00	105.00		40	40.00	820.00
15	15.00	120.00		41	41.00	861.00
16	16.00	136.00		42	42.00	903.00
17	17.00	153.00		43	43.00	946.00
18	18.00	171.00		44	44.00	990.00
19	19.00	190.00		45	45.00	1035.00
20	20.00	210.00		46	46.00	1081.00
21	21.00	231.00		47	47.00	1128.00
22	22.00	253.00		48	48.00	1176.00
23	23.00	276.00		49	49.00	1225.00
24	24.00	300.00		50	50.00	1275.00
25	25.00	325.00		51	51.00	1326.00
26	26.00	351.00		52	52.00	1378.00

The table above shows that you can save over $1,000 in one year with just a disciplined approach. The most you are saving in one week is $52.00.

The plan will change over time. Remember, I said it was a road map. When you plug a destination into your GPS, and then you run into traffic or an accident, you ask it to reroute you. It is the same with your budget. There may be times when you'll need to alter your budget as your life changes.

Remember what I said: slow and steady wins the race. It is about being disciplined. Doing the same thing all the time, every time. I'm not saying become boring and never have any fun. I think I've made it clear that fun should be a part of it. It's about having a plan for everything and following that plan.

Do you remember learning multiplication tables in school? We had to recite 2x2=4, 4x4=16, and so on. It was repetition. Everything in school, almost, is repetition. The more you do it, the more comfortable you become with it. The military is the same way. When you go into the army, they have you take your gun apart and put it back together a million times. Why? So you will get comfortable doing it and it will become second nature. You *will* become comfortable doing it.

Why do football teams run drills? So they will function as a team, become comfortable with each other, and memorize the plays. If the coach calls "Play A," everyone on that team understands what is about to happen on the field. If they change the play at the line, same thing – they all know that things have changed and now they will run the play that was called before the snap. What does all of this have to do with money? Well, you have to be ready for anything and everything. If your financial circumstances change, you need to have a plan for what to do.

You should be diverse in what you do. What do I mean by that? You should have some "money liquid" that you can get to in an emergency. You should have some "money after tax" invested. You should have some pretax money invested. You should own real-estate. You should own bonds, stocks, and mutual funds. I think everyone should play with a small account of an online brokerage account. You should not become obsessed with it. You should not put a ton of money in it, and I wouldn't become a day trader, but I think it's an awesome education on how the whole system works. It will give you confidence that you can read up on a company and learn how to buy, and when to sell, stocks. You could own shares in a local business. You could set up a foundation for something you are passionate about. It comes down to this: do your homework. Get with someone who is trained to look at the big picture. Again, ask for references before you start working with someone, and for pity's sake, don't turn over control to that person. It should be a partnership, not a takeover.

Let me share a story about this. In my hometown, there was a gentleman who owned a tax practice. He also did investing for his clients. He asked them to "loan" him money and he would give them a return of, say, ten percent over a year. Well, that was attractive to people, because rates, as you know, are not great with banks. Well, several people "loaned/invested" with him. And, as Paul Harvey had said, the rest of the story is that he was running a "Ponzi scheme," like Bernie Madoff, and people lost their entire retirement savings. He took, in excess of, twelve million dollars. In the beginning, he had done what he had promised: he paid them back with interest, and that spurred them to invest again, and now folks are having to start all over again. Just as a side note: there is no recourse for this. They sold his estate, but he had not used the money to buy assets. He had blown it. He had used it to go on vacations, and buy vacations for family members. So there was no money to give back to people. These people get to take it off their taxes, but that doesn't put the money back into their retirement accounts or their child's college funds.

So, again, it should be a partnership. Make sure your partner is investing you in reputable things and not just "borrowing" money from you.

5. HAPPILY EVER AFTER – DARE TO DREAM

Vision without action is a daydream. Action without vision is a nightmare (Japanese Proverb).

Food for thought…Thoughts are the beginning. Thoughts become words, and words become deeds. Deeds become habits, and habits shape the future.

No bank robber ever just wakes up one morning and decides to rob a bank. It starts with a thought. He walked into the bank one morning and looked at the teller line and the door, then thought, "It might be kind of easy to rob this bank." He returned a week later and looked at the cameras. He noticed where they were placed and thought, "How can I come into this bank without being noticed?" Still later, he thought, "I think I can go into the branch in a certain way that will keep my face non-visible, slip the teller a note, and be out the same way I came in, with my head down." He began to watch the flow and volume of the branch from the parking lot. One day, he walks in and robs the bank. And it all started with a single thought.

Now, I've just given you a bad scenario for how thought starts the ball rolling. What I want you to do is use this "thought philosophy" to improve your life. Start to think about where you want to go in your life. Take the blinders off; dream as if you have a million dollars. In fact, play that game too. What would you do with a million dollars? Write it down. *Write it down.* I had to do this in fifth grade. It was really hard, as a fifth grader, to imagine how I would spend a million dollars as an adult. I had to buy a home, furnishings, and things for my children and family. It was a hard thing to imagine then, but now, well, now it's a blast. It's about possibilities. What is possible?

He who fails to plan, plans to fail – Proverb

Imagination is more important than knowledge – Einstein

"We are what we think. All that we are arises with our thoughts. With our thoughts, we make the world" – Buddha

"Thinking: The talking of the soul with itself" – Plato

The most pathetic person in the world is someone with sight but no vision – Helen Keller

Everything begins as a dream. Ask any successful person and they will tell you that they saw the possibility from a dream.

Let's talk about someone in modern day who has had a dream become a reality: Tyler Perry. He was homeless and went from that situation to one of the most sought after people in America. He's built Tyler Perry Studios from the ground up – all because he had a dream. He took all the money he had and rented a venue to put on a play that he had no idea anyone would come to. But he did it anyway.

Do you remember, as a child, daydreaming about what you wanted to be when you grew up? Do you remember dreaming about places you wanted to see and live at? Well, those were not pipe dreams. As children, we do not have all the clutter in our minds that adults do. You know, those thoughts of words that people have told you all your life…you will never amount to anything…you can't open that business…you can't retire at forty-five – unless you invent something like Facebook. Well, I am here to tell you, if you will get back to dreaming, you will see that anything is possible.

Why do people stop dreaming? Failure? Fear? Dreams in the past not coming fast enough, or not at all? The problem with all of these excuses is, if you stop because of one of them, you will never see your dream become a reality, because you didn't put forth the effort to make it happen. They are only excuses, caused by the "what ifs." Do you realize that statistics tell us that eighty percent of what we worry about *never happens*? So it's time to lay down the excuses and pick up a pen.

Let me go back to my divorce for a second. When I realized that I was going to be starting over again, I was crushed. I felt as though I had just begun to reach the time in my life that I had dreamed about. I had a place to entertain people. I had, what appeared to be, the Ken and Barbie marriage. I had friends. I had climbed the corporate ladder long enough to realize that I didn't want to climb any higher because of the ceiling that was present. I wanted to – and did – branch out on my own with my best friend, Tonya, and started an accounting firm. I was now looking at that whole dream that had become a nightmare.

Life is funny. Just when you think it's over, spring comes again and everything begins again – birth happens, new beginnings start.

One thing I stopped doing in the last months of my marriage and the first year of my new life was dream. I was hurt; I was embarrassed; I had been rejected; and I had given up on trusting anyone. As the pity party for myself became old, I began to look around and remembered a wise man who had once told me that, for something to happen, I needed to write it down. Not just for the current year, but for five years out and ten years out. I found the recording I'd had of that and began to listen to it. For one week I listened to it going to and coming from work. I began the process of healing and began to dream again. I began to write things down.

I created a wish book. I began to write down how I wanted to look, where I wanted to live, how much money I wanted to make, where I wanted to travel. It took a huge leap of faith for me to begin to put those things on paper. I was still paying for medical bills from my health insurance being cancelled. I was about to have to split the equity of a home that I had made most of the payments for. It was, at that time, when I really had to talk to the person in the mirror. I had to forgive and forget. I had to place my thoughts on the moment and the future. It was the hardest thing in my life I'd ever done.

Something happened. I began to believe again. I began to get my confidence back.

That first year, I wrote down things like:

- Exercise everyday
- Make enough money to pay my bills and save for retirement
- Go on a vacation
- Remodel my new house (it was built in 1950 and was in need of updating)

The next year I added:

- Get married
- Have a family
- Have the same – or greater – net worth than I'd had previously

Why am I telling you this? I want you to do the same thing. I don't care if you buy a journal or a spiral-bound notebook. Just do it!

I read a story once about a man who wrote down a "life list." He listed many things that he wanted to do in his life. Do you know that he completed most of what he had written down? Scientists tell us that we are fifty percent more likely to complete the things that we write down. It's a law – like gravity.

Here is a breakdown of what you should include in your list:

- How do you want to look physically?
- How much money do you want to make?

- How much money do you want to give away?
- Where do you want to live?
- Do you want to return or start going to school?
- Where do you want to vacation?
- How much money do you want to save?

Let your imagination run wild. Pretend you are a child again and just see what happens. Retirement isn't the time to do what you've always dreamed of doing. Nor is it the time to put your purpose and gift to work. Do it now. If you can't do it right now, put it on paper and move in that direction. I am living proof that if you take the time to do this, it will change you forever.

Our Founding Fathers put down on paper what they wanted this nation to look like. Do you know we are the only nation with the oldest Constitution that's still in use? This document was planned to stand the tests of time.

Your life's vision should do the same. No one should be able to overtake your dreams. You should be the master of your fate and the captain of your soul. You can also be your own worst enemy. You have to silence that voice inside your head that says, "I'll never get ahead. I'll fail again. I'll never be able to save a million dollars." Let's go back to what I said earlier in the book about the runner. If you've never run before, how do you know what you are capable of? What if our Founding Fathers had taken that approach? What if they had looked at other countries and said, "No one has had a constitution last any length of time so it must not be possible." For those of you who are married, what if the Founding Fathers, who had all come from different backgrounds and philosophies, had not come together as a team and created our nation? I know it sounds simple – that's because it is! It is a decision. Companies do it all the time. They set out goals for the company. Most of the time those companies are comprised of different people on a board, with different objectives, but they manage to create a vision for their company and they succeed. In my experience, the people and companies I have seen fail did so, because they did not handle money well. And they didn't have a vision.

Your life should be able to be measured. We know that there are sixty seconds in a minute, sixty minutes in an hour, and three hundred sixty-five days in a year. So, as we count those things, we should count our lives. This is another reason you need to dream and you need to have a vision. If you don't, how will you know what you've accomplished? I am not just talking about where money is concerned. I am talking about life in general. You should be able to measure how your life is going. Here's a great example. Most women I know monitor their weight. You hear them talk about what they weighed in high school, college, before a baby, after a baby, and so on. They are measuring how it changes over time. Athletes do something similar. The first day they train for a marathon, they don't run the entire distance; they start out with a much shorter distance and measure their progress over a period of time as the race day approaches.

The Founding Fathers were about measuring things. Franklin kept a record of all he had invented. It took Edison over two thousand tries to create the light bulb. He recorded them all, so he knew what to do different the next time. He said, after all those tries, he didn't fail; he just found two thousand ways how not to make a light bulb. When creating the nation, they had a vision. They wanted it to be unlike anything that ever existed before. They took that vision and constructed our constitution from it. Why do we think we should stop visioning or dreaming? We were designed for greatness. All that is stopping us is us.

As I end the book, let me leave you with my life story. In doing so, I hope you will see that if I can do it, so can you. I shared with you that I got remarried 34 I didn't tell you that ninety days after I got married, I quit my $80,000 a year job to start my own company. I made $8,000 that first year. To say that I was quite freaked out was an understatement. Here I was, newly married, and I had put a financial strain (or so I had thought) on my marriage. During this time, I remembered a test the bank had us take that showed major stressors in your life. Getting married was one; losing a job was another (or reduction in income). Here I had two of those major stressors, within ninety days of saying "I do," *but* we had a plan. We didn't miss a beat. We were making two house payments at that time, because we had not yet rented my house. Before we said "I do," I took a class about purpose and discovered that what I had been doing on the side my whole adult life was my gift, and I needed to move in that direction. So, while I was freaked out, I had a calmness that I had never known. I had taken flight, and it only took thirty-four years to do it.

Over the next two years, my business income doubled each year. I dared to dream. I asked myself, "What would it look like if I owned my own business?" I wrote down a plan and began to walk that plan out. I began to stop being afraid of failure and began to live.

Now, the last nine years have not all been rosy. I rented business space from someone who took advantage of my kindness and my naivety in business. Once burned, twice shy. I also learned that contracts are good things. There was one thing I didn't plan for: people not paying. I had to adjust for that and not count on all the money coming in like it was supposed to. I had to learn how to collect when someone didn't pay. Contracts are a good thing, even between people you know. It keeps the emotion out of it, just like a budget does.

I wrote "Money 101." I started looking for places to teach. The first time I taught it, I had four people attend. I've now taught it to as many as one hundred at a time. I have been blessed to have companies ask me to come teach their employees (at the company's expense). I have worked with couples, single people, and students.

While I dreamed all of this, I wrote it down. It still seems so unreal sometimes. I am getting to live out what I had wrote down. So, you see, I'm not asking you to do something I haven't lived. I'm not going to tell you it's an easy road. It takes work. It takes dedication. But you can do it!

CONCLUSION

You may be thinking, "She's asking a lot." I guess, if you see this as a mountain, I am. Remember, how do you eat an elephant? One bite at a time. Sit down and begin one step at a time. Daydream a little bit. Write down some things on paper that you want to see, do, be, and have. From there, start working on your budget. Just take the first step and it will fall into place. I have had people who've left my Money 101 class, took these steps, and emailed me to tell me that they slept the very best that they have in years, just from getting their budget complete. Knowing where you are will bring you peace of mind about the present, and having a vision will bring you peace of mind about your future.

Once you complete those steps, it will be easier to resist the pressure from our current culture to keep up with the Jones'. That rollercoaster is one that is not fun to ride. Don't let peer pressure tell you what you should have, do, or be. We are a unique nation and each one of us is unique in our own right. We need to be about the business of becoming what we were born to be and not trying to conform to a system that is designed to enslave us – a system that is designed to have us purchase things that will wear out before we have paid for them.

I have heard all my life that you have to pay your dues. I firmly believe that in this aspect. We need to have our ducks in a row before we launch out into something. Just imagine, for a minute, how our nation would look if everyone did that? There would be no housing crisis. Bankruptcy would be a thing of the past. The mass amounts of things dumped into a landfill would be minimized. We wouldn't go through things like water, just because it is what the culture says we should do.

Imagine how much more peaceful we would be as human beings, if we weren't always worried about what people thought of us or if they approved of where we were in life. It's our life. We should be measuring it, not having someone else tell us our worth because we don't have the same path. The one constant thing we should all have in common is a dream and a plan, and working on both.

We should be cheering each other on for becoming financially independent. Instead, if you watch our culture, it says we should always have debt. We should always be trying to reach that next level, and we should always be striving for something – something that makes us better people.

When Neo took the red pill and went down the rabbit hole, it wasn't an easy journey. But it was real. It was his life, his way. He realized that the rollercoaster was safe to get off, once it had stopped. He realized that there was more to life than just having a mediocre job. There was greatness in him. Zion was waiting for him to become what he was born to be.

Our nation, this planet, is waiting on you to become what you were born to be…We the People. It is waiting on you to get a plan and work it – without fear of others, failure, or anything that could happen. I think of Nelson Mandela. He was imprisoned for a long time, and when he came out, he changed the world. So, no matter where you are, no matter what has happened to you, no matter what mistakes you've made, as long as you are still breathing, you can change things. You can start today and live a different life than you have been living. A life of freedom.

If this book has helped you, I'd love to hear from you. Please email me.

MONEY NUGGETS

- If you add just one-hundred dollars to each house payment you make, you will pay off your house in one-half the amount of time that you financed it for. Something that simple can cut fifteen years off a thirty-year mortgage.

- Shop insurance for your home and automobiles. You will be amazed at the differences. Make sure you compare apples to apples. Some companies offer great rates and skimp on coverage. Do your homework.

- Consider a higher deductible on some policies to save cost. *Make sure you have the deductible* in an account so you will have it when and if you need it.

- Don't buy groceries when you're hungry.

- Make a list for the store. Take the time to plan out your meals for the one or two-week period. List those things that you need to make those meals. *Stick to the list!*

- Cook at home. Not only is it healthier for you, but it will save you money in the long run.

- Take your lunch to work. This could save you $1,300 a year (if you purchase a food-like substance from a fast food place and spend $5.00 for the meal).

- If you have problems saving money, have a savings account with a different bank. Don't get a debit/ATM card with it, so it will be more difficult for you to withdraw from it.

- Learn to shop store sales. Everything goes on sale. It's about timing. Find a clerk in your favorite store and ask them when it will be on sale. They know. And they will share that information with you. There is nothing (to me) more satisfying than buying that dress or shoes or purse at fifty to seventy-five percent off!

- Create a budget for remodeling, even if it's just new linens and paint for the bedroom. This will prevent you from overspending, and if you shop around and write it all down on paper before you start the project, there won't –shouldn't – be any surprises.

- Check out websites like Groupon, Living Social, and Restaurant.com for entertainment savings.

- This may step on some toes, but stop buying carbonated drinks. Drink water instead. This will make you healthier and it will be healthier for your finances too.

- When going out, plan your route. With gas at $3.50 a gallon, this is almost a must. Go to the store on your lunch break or on the way home from work. Plan your route so you can do all that you need to do in one trip. It will save you on gas and operating costs for your vehicle.

- Keep up the maintenance on your vehicle. It will last longer and be more efficient.

- Buy a programmable thermostat for your home. When you aren't there, don't keep it as cool or as warm as when you are at home. This will save you in electrical and maintenance costs. In the winter, keep your house at sixty-eight degrees. This can save you a couple of percent on your bill. If you program it to fifty-five degrees when you aren't at home, you can see a twenty-plus percent savings.

- Plan vacations in advance. Visit websites like Vrbo.com and Kayak.com. With Vrbo.com, you are renting from the owner. Kayak.com will compare rates for you. Check the fine print. If you know which dates you're going, sometimes you will get a deal just for booking and paying (non-refundable) at the time of booking.

- Pay for as much as you can with cash. There is a chemical reaction that happens when you do this that does not happen when you pay with credit. It also makes you aware of how much you are spending.

- Never make a big purchase – my rule is anything over one-hundred dollars – on impulse. Sleep on it.

- Shop healthcare options. When looking for a doctor, it pays to call and ask questions. If you have a high-deductible insurance plan, this will help you keep those costs in check.

- There is an app for that. Check out free apps for coupons, sales, and gas prices. These can help you plan your route, and save you money too.

- Gym membership – Ask lots of questions. If you have a contract, how long is it for? What are the fees to cancel? Do they have a month-to-month or per-visit payment schedule? Is it cheaper for you to have an app on your tablet or phone, where you can do exercises at home?

- I realize we live in a download culture, but there is still a thing called a library, which is cheaper (as long as you return on time) than downloading a new book on your Kindle, Nook, or tablet.

- Check out the free books you can download from different book websites. Usually there is a free-book weekly. These may not be on the best-seller list but may still be a great read.

- Eliminate late fees by paying your bills on time. This can save you thousands.

- Manage your tax liability well. The goal is to owe nothing and to get nothing back. I know that's a shock. So if you are getting a large refund each year, consider adding an exemption to your W-4 and take more money home with you throughout the year. You aren't gaining anything by the government holding your money for a year.

This is by no means an all-inclusive list. It's just some things I've seen work over time. Every little bit helps.

ABOUT THE AUTHOR

Stephanie Dickert is an entrepreneur and owner of "Stewardship for Life," an accounting firm. She is a reformed banker-turned-accountant. She also developed "Money 101," because of a need she saw in society for money management made simple. She challenges people to live life to the fullest, simply, and in the moment. Stephanie loves teaching Money 101, and offers classes quarterly and for corporate America, as requested. She has appeared on several talk shows about money management and living life in balance. She is a sought-after motivational speaker. She is passionate about helping people live life with the purpose that they were born with. She's a wife and mother, and an avid farmer.

Stephanie helped get the Tennessee Home School bill passed in the eighties. At thirteen, she had the privilege of speaking to the House and the Senate regarding the bill.

She's traveled in most of the United States, Europe, and Mexico. She is forever looking for new perspectives on money habits and how cultures influence us.

Visit her website at:

www.stewardshipforlife.net

And her blog at:

www.differentperspectivelife.blogspot.com.

Made in the USA
Monee, IL
08 November 2026

67967620R00049